## F HORN

# MOVIE FAVORITES

*Solos and Band Arrangements*
*Correlated with Essential Elements Band Method*

## Arranged by
## MICHAEL SWEENEY

Welcome to Essential Elements Movie Favorites! There are two versions of each selection in this versatile book. The SOLO version appears on the left-hand page of your book. The FULL BAND arrangement appears on the right-hand page. Optional accompaniment recordings are available separately in CD or cassette format. Use these recordings when playing solos for friends and family.

ISBN 978-0-7935-5962-6

HAL•LEONARD®
CORPORATION

7777 W. BLUEMOUND RD. P.O. BOX 13819 MILWAUKEE, WI 53213

00860018

**From The Universal Motion Picture JURASSIC PARK**

# Theme From "JURASSIC PARK"

**F HORN**
Solo

**Composed by JOHN WILLIAMS**
**Arranged by MICHAEL SWEENEY**

**MCA** music publishing

00860018

# Theme From "JURASSIC PARK"

**F HORN**
**Band Arrangement**

**Composed by JOHN WILLIAMS**
Arranged by MICHAEL SWEENEY

**MCA** music publishing

**From CHARIOTS OF FIRE**

# CHARIOTS OF FIRE

F HORN
Solo

**Music by VANGELIS**
Arranged by MICHAEL SWEENEY

# CHARIOTS OF FIRE

**F HORN**
**Band Arrangement**

Music by VANGELIS
Arranged by MICHAEL SWEENEY

00860018

From THE MAN FROM SNOWY RIVER

# THE MAN FROM SNOWY RIVER
### (Main Title Theme)

F HORN
Solo

By BRUCE ROWLAND
Arranged by MICHAEL SWEENEY

# THE MAN FROM SNOWY RIVER
### (Main Title Theme)

F HORN
Band Arrangement

By BRUCE ROWLAND
Arranged by MICHAEL SWEENEY

00860018

**From The Paramount Motion Picture FORREST GUMP**

# FORREST GUMP - MAIN TITLE
### (Feather Theme)

Music by ALAN SILVESTRI
Arranged by MICHAEL SWEENEY

F HORN
Solo

00860018

From The Paramount Motion Picture FORREST GUMP

# FORREST GUMP - MAIN TITLE

(Feather Theme)

F HORN
Band Arrangement

**Music by ALAN SILVESTRI**
Arranged by MICHAEL SWEENEY

00860018

**From AN AMERICAN TAIL**
# SOMEWHERE OUT THERE

Words and Music by JAMES HORNER,
BARRY MANN and CYNTHIA WEIL
Arranged by MICHAEL SWEENEY

F HORN
Solo

**MCA** music publishing

00860018

# From AN AMERICAN TAIL
# SOMEWHERE OUT THERE

**Words and Music by JAMES HORNER,
BARRY MANN and CYNTHIA WEIL**
Arranged by MICHAEL SWEENEY

F HORN
Band Arrangement

**MCA** music publishing

00860018

From **DANCES WITH WOLVES**
# THE JOHN DUNBAR THEME

F HORN
Solo

By **JOHN BARRY**
Arranged by **MICHAEL SWEENEY**

**From DANCES WITH WOLVES**

# THE JOHN DUNBAR THEME

**F HORN**
**Band Arrangement**

**By JOHN BARRY**
Arranged by MICHAEL SWEENEY

00860018

**From The Paramount Motion Picture RAIDERS OF THE LOST ARK**

# RAIDERS MARCH

**By JOHN WILLIAMS**
Arranged by MICHAEL SWEENEY

F HORN
Solo

**From The Paramount Motion Picture RAIDERS OF THE LOST ARK**

# RAIDERS MARCH

F HORN
Band Arrangement

By JOHN WILLIAMS
Arranged by MICHAEL SWEENEY

00860018

From APOLLO 13
# APOLLO 13
(End Credits)

By JAMES HORNER
Arranged by MICHAEL SWEENEY

F HORN
Solo

MCA music publishing

# APOLLO 13
### (End Credits)

**F HORN**
**Band Arrangement**

By JAMES HORNER
Arranged by MICHAEL SWEENEY

**MCA** music publishing

00860018

From The Universal Picture E.T. (THE EXTRA-TERRESTRIAL)

# THEME FROM E.T. (THE EXTRA-TERRESTRIAL)

F HORN
Solo

Music by JOHN WILLIAMS
Arranged by MICHAEL SWEENEY

MCA music publishing

# THEME FROM E.T. (THE EXTRA-TERRESTRIAL)

F HORN
Band Arrangement

Music by JOHN WILLIAMS
Arranged by MICHAEL SWEENEY

MCA music publishing

**Theme From The Paramount Picture STAR TREK**

# STAR TREK®-THE MOTION PICTURE

F HORN
Solo

Music by JERRY GOLDSMITH
Arranged by MICHAEL SWEENEY

# STAR TREK®-THE MOTION PICTURE

F HORN
Band Arrangement

**Music by JERRY GOLDSMITH**
Arranged by MICHAEL SWEENEY

Moderate March

**From The Universal Motion Picture BACK TO THE FUTURE**

# BACK TO THE FUTURE

**By ALAN SILVESTRI**
Arranged by MICHAEL SWEENEY

F HORN
Solo

MCA music publishing

# BACK TO THE FUTURE

F HORN
Band Arrangement

By ALAN SILVESTRI
Arranged by MICHAEL SWEENEY

MCA music publishing